THE ULTIMATE REAL ESTATE GUIDE

BY

DAVID S PHUNG

Boris E. Vasquez, Contributor

Sheng Yen, Contributor

Aaron Lee, Assistant Contributor

Alejandra Acosta, Assistant Contributor

David S Phung, Author

Boris E. Vasquez, Contributor

Sheng Yen, Contributor

Aaron Lee, Assistant Contributor

Alejandra Acosta, Assistant Contributor

David S Phung, M.S., Realtor
DRE # 01741202
LPT Realty, Inc.

Boris E. Vasquez, Real Estate Broker, Contributor
Real Estate, Mortgage & Tax Consultant
DRE # 02015972
NMLS # 1520547
CTEC # A357742

Sheng Yen, Contributor
DRE # 02007399
eXp Realty of California, Inc.

Aaron Lee, Assistant **Contributor**
DRE: 01439455
Keller Williams Realty

Alejandra Acosta, Assistant Contributor,
Transaction Manager
AC Professional Transactions

Author's Introduction

David S Phung is a seasoned real estate professional whose career reflects a rare blend of dedication, entrepreneurial vision, and a strong commitment to empowering others through knowledge. Based in Sacramento, California, David has become a trusted advisor to both clients and colleagues, renowned for his integrity, market expertise, and personalized service.

Currently an agent with LPT Realty, Inc., David's professional journey includes roles at some of the most respected brokerages in the industry: Keller Williams Realty, eXp Realty, and Berkshire Hathaway Home Services. He has dedicated his career to helping clients successfully navigate the real estate market, consistently ensuring their needs and ambitions remain his top priority.

David's dedication to the profession is underscored by his active membership in the Sacramento Association of Realtors, the California Association of Realtors, and the National Association of Realtors. His commitment was recognized with a Certificate of Appreciation from the Realtor Action Fund Investor in 2009, a testament to his contributions to the real estate community and his advocacy for responsible homeownership.

Professional Experience

David's professional background extends beyond real estate, reflecting his lifelong dedication to service and entrepreneurship. He began his career with the City of Sacramento's Central Services and its Summer Youth Employment Training Program, where he developed a strong foundation in public service and community engagement.

In 1990, David's entrepreneurial spirit led him to establish Victor Printing, his own business, which he successfully operated for nearly five years. This experience honed his skills in operations, customer relations, and strategic growth, strengths he continues to apply in his real estate practice today.

Over the years, David has collaborated with a wide network of real estate professionals, including loan officers, escrow and title companies, repair specialists, and inspection teams, as well as other key industry entities. This extensive collaboration has equipped him with a well-rounded understanding of the real estate process and earned him a reputation for delivering smooth, efficient transactions for his clients.

Education

David's academic achievements form the backbone of his professional excellence. He holds a Master of Science in Management Information Systems with a focus on Project Management from Golden Gate University, Sacramento Campus, San Francisco, CA. Additionally, he earned dual Bachelor of Science degrees from California State University, Sacramento, one in Business Administration (Strategic Management/Operations Management) and another in Graphic Design/Marketing.

He is also a proud graduate of the Sacramento Entrepreneurship Academy, where he earned a diploma in Entrepreneurship in 1997. David further expanded his expertise through participation in national leadership programs, including the U.S. Minority Business Development Agency's Emerging Business Leader Summit in Washington, D.C., and the U.S. Small Business Administration's 50-Year National Conference in Bay Lake, Florida.

A Message to Readers

Through this book, David S Phung shares practical guidance, proven strategies, and insider perspectives drawn from decades of real-world experience. His goal is simple yet powerful: to equip you, whether you are a first-time homebuyer, seasoned investor, or aspiring real estate professional, with the insights and confidence you need to make smart, informed decisions in today's ever-changing market.

David's story reminds us that success in real estate, as in life, is built on a foundation of knowledge, integrity, and a genuine commitment to serving others. May his journey and expertise inspire you as you embark on your path to real estate success.

Disclaimer

This book was written to share practical advice, proven strategies, personal experiences, and honest insights into the world of real estate. Whether you're an investor, agent, buyer, or seller, the goal is to help you make more informed decisions, avoid common pitfalls, and approach real estate with clarity and confidence.

That said, the information in this book is for educational and informational purposes only. Real estate markets, laws, and regulations vary by location and can change over time. What works well in one situation may not apply in another. For that reason, nothing in this book should be considered legal, financial, or tax advice.

Before making any real estate decisions, whether buying, selling, investing, or applying a technique from this book, we strongly recommend consulting with qualified professionals, including real estate attorneys, licensed agents, tax advisors, or financial planners.

While every effort has been made to ensure the accuracy and usefulness of the content, neither the author nor the publisher can be held legally or professionally liable for any actions taken based on the material provided.

Use this book as a trusted guide, but always do your due diligence. Your choices are your responsibility, and your success comes from combining knowledge with good judgment and expert support.

Introduction

1. Story and Expertise

   - Brief personal introduction and professional background in real estate.

   - Why did you write this book, and how can it help readers achieve their real estate goals?

2. Who This Book is For

   - First-time buyers, sellers, and those interested in profiting from real estate.

   - Professionals and aspiring investors looking for practical advice and guidance.

3. What Readers Will Learn

   - Step-by-step processes for buying and selling homes.

   - Tips for profiting from real estate investments.

   - Unique strategies that set this book apart from others.

Book Outline:

Part 1: Buying Real Estate (1/3 Focus)

1. Understanding the Real Estate Market

   - Overview of market trends, buyer behavior, and how to read the market.

2. Steps to Buying Your Dream Home

   - Budgeting and getting pre-approved for a mortgage.

   - Choosing the right location and property type.

3. Working with Real Estate Professionals

   - Role of agents, brokers, and other specialists.

   - How to find and evaluate a good real estate agent.

4. The Home Buying Process

   - Making offers, negotiating, and closing deals.

   - Home inspections, appraisals, and paperwork essentials.

5. Mistakes to Avoid When Buying

   - Common pitfalls and how to steer clear of them.

Part 2: Selling Real Estate (2/3 Focus)

1. Why Selling Real Estate is an Art

   - Importance of presentation, marketing, and timing.

2. Steps to Successfully Selling a Home

   - Preparing your home for sale (staging, repairs, and curb appeal).

   - Setting the right price: How to determine market value.

3. Effective Marketing Techniques

   - Online and offline marketing strategies.

   - Using social media, professional photography, and virtual tours.

4. Working with an Agent to List Your Home

   - What to expect and how to collaborate for the best results.

   - Choosing the right agent for your needs.

5. Negotiation and Closing

   - How to handle offers, counteroffers, and closing processes.

6. Profiting from Real Estate Sales

   - Strategies for maximizing returns on your property.

   - Tax implications and how to reinvest profits.

Conclusion

1. Recap of Key Points

   - Summarizing the buying, selling, and investing processes.

2. Next Steps for Readers

   - Encouraging readers to take action and apply the strategies.

3. Resources and Tools

   - List of helpful resources, websites, and contact information.

TABLE OF CONTENTS:

Part 1

Buying Real Estate

(1/3 Focus)

Chapter 1

Decoding the Real Estate Market: Where to Begin

The real estate market can feel overwhelming, especially for first-time buyers, but building a solid understanding of the fundamentals is key to navigating it with confidence. By learning how to interpret market trends, recognize buyer behavior, and identify key indicators, you'll be better equipped to make informed decisions. With the right knowledge, what once seemed complex becomes manageable, empowering you to move forward in your real estate journey with clarity and assurance.

Understanding the California Real Estate Transaction Timeline and Process

In a standard California real estate transaction, the entire process, including escrow and closing, typically spans 30 to 60 days. However, this timeline can fluctuate depending on various factors such as the transaction's complexity, the buyer's financing arrangements, and any contingencies outlined in the purchase agreement.

General Timeline Overview:

Pre-Contract Phase: This stage involves negotiations and offers leading up to the signing of the purchase agreement.

Due Diligence Phase: During this period, the buyer conducts inspections and confirms the property's title and condition.

Financing Phase: The buyer works on securing mortgage approval.

Escrow and Closing: An escrow company holds funds, documents, and instructions until all contract conditions are satisfied, culminating in the legal transfer of ownership.

Key Timeframes During the Transaction:

Initial Offer: The buyer submits an offer to purchase the property. Escrow Duration: Generally, it lasts between 30 to 60 days.

Property Inspections: Buyers usually have 17 days to complete inspections.

Loan Application: Buyers are typically expected to submit loan applications within 7 days.

Disclosures: Sellers generally provide all required disclosures within 7 days.

Closing: The closing process typically takes several days and is often handled through digital platforms.

Factors That May Impact the Timeline:

Transaction Complexity: Transactions involving commercial properties, probate sales, or multiple owners may require additional time.

Buyer's Financing: Delays in mortgage approval can extend the overall process.

Contractual Contingencies: If the buyer includes contingencies (e.g., home inspection or appraisal), the closing may be delayed to allow time for resolution.

Communication and Coordination: Smooth and timely communication among all parties, buyers, sellers, agents, escrow officers, and lenders can help accelerate the transaction.

Important Considerations:

"Time is of the Essence" Clause: Most contracts include this clause, emphasizing the importance of meeting all deadlines.

Contingency Removals: Any contingency removals must be documented in writing.

Notice to Perform: If one party fails to meet a deadline, the other party may issue a "Notice to Perform" to prompt action.

Digital Closings: The use of digital platforms for signing and processing documents is on the rise and can significantly streamline the closing process.

The Real Estate Market Landscape

Real estate is dynamic, with fluctuations influenced by various factors such as economic conditions, interest rates, and local developments. For instance, during economic booms, property prices tend to rise as demand increases. Conversely, in slower economies, prices may stabilize or even drop. Monitoring these trends can help you time your purchase strategically.

One way to gain insights is through market reports and indexes. Websites like Zillow, Redfin, or local Multiple Listing Services (MLS) offer data on median home prices, inventory levels, and days on market. Pay attention to whether it's a buyer's or seller's market. In a buyer's market, you have more negotiating power due to higher inventory levels, while in a seller's market, competition can drive up prices.

Buyer Behavior and Its Implications

Understanding how buyers behave in the market can offer valuable cues. For example, families often prioritize school districts, while young professionals might focus on urban areas with shorter commutes. By identifying your priorities, you can align your search with similar market segments.

Additionally, seasonality plays a role. Spring and summer are typically peak seasons for home buying, which can lead to higher competition. If you're looking for better deals, consider searching during off-peak seasons like fall or winter.

Reading the Market Effectively

Reading the market involves more than just tracking prices. Look for trends like gentrification, upcoming infrastructure projects, or zoning changes that might increase property values. For example, a new transit line could make a neighborhood more accessible and desirable.

Attend open houses and talk to local agents to gather firsthand insights. Comparing similar properties in your preferred area, a process known as "comps," can also help you determine fair market value. Tools like property history records reveal how much a home has appreciated over time, providing clues about its investment potential.

By mastering these basics, you're well on your way to making smarter decisions in the real estate market.

Chapter 2

Your Dream Home Starts Here: Budgeting and Financing

Embarking on the journey to buy your dream home starts with careful financial planning. Budgeting and securing financing are essential steps that lay the groundwork for a smooth purchasing process. By setting realistic expectations and exploring your options, you can ensure your dream home fits within your financial means.

Setting Your Budget

Before diving into listings, assess your financial health. This includes calculating your savings, monthly income, and expenses. A general rule is to allocate no more than 28% of your gross income to housing costs, including mortgage payments, property taxes, and insurance.

Don't forget additional costs such as closing fees, moving expenses, and ongoing maintenance. Creating a comprehensive budget ensures you're not caught off guard by unexpected expenses. Online calculators can help you estimate monthly payments based on your loan amount, interest rate, and term length.

Getting Pre-Approved for a Mortgage

A pre-approval letter from a lender not only clarifies your borrowing capacity but also signals to sellers that you're a serious buyer. During pre-approval, lenders evaluate your credit score, debt-to-income (DTI) ratio, and employment history. Aim for a credit score of at least

620 to qualify for most conventional loans, though higher scores often lead to better terms.

Research different mortgage types, such as fixed-rate, adjustable-rate, or FHA loans, to determine which suits your situation best. Fixed-rate mortgages provide stability with consistent payments, while adjustable-rate mortgages may start lower but fluctuate over time.

Choosing the Right Financing Option

Beyond traditional mortgages, explore programs for first-time buyers or veterans, which may offer lower down payments or interest rates. Additionally, some states provide assistance programs or tax credits to ease the financial burden.

If possible, aim to put down at least 20% of the home's price to avoid private mortgage insurance (PMI), which can add to your monthly costs. However, many lenders now offer low-down-payment options for qualified buyers.

Saving for the Down Payment

Building your down payment requires discipline and planning. Consider setting up a dedicated savings account and automating contributions. Cut back on discretionary spending or find additional income sources to reach your goal faster.

There are also creative ways to save, such as leveraging employer-sponsored homeownership programs or using gifted funds from family. Just ensure any large deposits are documented to satisfy lender requirements.

Evaluating Affordability

Once pre-approved, compare your budget against actual home prices in your target areas. While it's tempting to stretch for a dream property, staying within your means ensures financial stability. Remember, your dream home should enhance your life, not strain your finances.

By taking these steps, you'll be well-prepared to move forward in the home-buying process, armed with the confidence that your finances are in order.

Chapter 3

The Perfect Match: Finding the Right Agent and Property

Buying a home is a major life decision. It's not just about finding a house, it's about finding the right home: a place where you feel safe, comfortable, and happy. But before you step into your dream home, you need two things: a great real estate agent and the perfect property.

This chapter will guide you through the process of choosing a reliable agent and identifying the right property that aligns with your needs, budget, and long-term goals.

The Role of a Real Estate Agent: Your Trusted Guide

A good real estate agent is like a matchmaker. They don't just show you houses, they listen to your needs, understand your financial situation, and guide you toward properties that complement your lifestyle.

Why You Need a Good Agent:

Expert Knowledge: Real estate agents understand market trends, pricing strategies, and the best neighborhoods.

Negotiation Skills: They help you secure the best deal by negotiating with sellers.

Legal Guidance: They manage contracts, ensuring your paperwork is complete and accurate.

Access to More Listings: Many properties aren't publicly listed, but agents have access to exclusive deals.

Saves Time and Stress: Instead of browsing endlessly, your agent filters options based on your preferences.

How to Choose the Right Agent:

Not all agents are created equal. Some have more experience, while others specialize in certain types of properties. Here's how to find your ideal match:

Check Their Experience: Look for agents with a solid track record in your preferred area.

Read Reviews and Ask for Referrals: Online reviews and recommendations from friends can help you identify trusted professionals.

Interview Multiple Agents: Don't settle for the first one you meet. Ask about their process, fees, and success rate.

Assess Their Communication Skills: A good agent should be accessible, honest, and patient when answering your questions.

Once you've found a dependable agent, it's time to clarify what you're looking for in a property.

Identifying Your Dream Home: What Matters Most?

Before you start viewing homes, define your priorities. Consider these essential factors:

1. Your Budget

Determine how much you can realistically afford. Include: Your savings for a down payment.

Your mortgage eligibility.

Additional expenses like taxes, insurance, and upkeep.

2. Type of Property

Single-family home: Great for privacy and space.

Apartment or condo: Ideal for city living with lower maintenance. Townhouse: A compromise between a house and an apartment.

3. Location Matters

Think about:

Commute time: How far is it from work, school, or daily destinations? Amenities: Are supermarkets, hospitals, or parks nearby?

Neighborhood safety: Research crime rates and read community reviews.

4. Must-Have Features

How many bedrooms and bathrooms do you need? Do you want a backyard, balcony, or garage?

Are you looking for a newly constructed home or one with historic charm?

Finding the Right Property

Once your priorities are clear, here's how to search efficiently:

Browse Online Listings: Websites like Zillow or Realtor.com offer photos, maps, and specs.

Visit Open Houses: This gives you a feel for both the property and its neighborhood.

Rely on Your Agent: They can uncover hidden gems and schedule private viewings.

Take Notes and Compare: After touring multiple homes, use a checklist to keep track of pros and cons.

Finalizing Your Choice

When you find a home you love, take these steps before making an offer:

- ✅ Visit it at different times. Observe noise levels, traffic, and the neighborhood vibe.

- ✅ Check the property's history. Ask about past repairs, renovations, or legal issues.

- ✅ Discuss with your agent. They can help you craft a competitive and informed offer.

Finding the right property is a balance of logic and emotion. Trust your instincts, but always do your own due diligence.

Chapter 4

From Offer to Ownership:

Navigating the Buying Process

Now that you've found the perfect home, it's time to turn that dream into reality.

But buying a house isn't as simple as handing over money and getting the keys. There are steps, paperwork, negotiations, and legal processes involved. This chapter will break it all down so you know exactly what to expect.

Step 1: Making an Offer

Your agent will help you prepare a formal offer. This includes:

- ✅ Your proposed price: Based on market value and the property's Condition.

- ✅ Contingencies: Conditions such as passing a home inspection or securing loan approval.

- ✅ Earnest Money Deposit: A small upfront amount to demonstrate you're serious.

What Happens Next?

The seller has three options:

Accept: Congratulations! You move to the next step.

Counteroffer: They may negotiate for a higher price or more favorable terms.

Reject: If this happens, you can submit a new offer or search for another property.

Step 2: Home Inspection & Appraisal

Once your offer is accepted, these two evaluations help ensure you're making a sound investment. Home Inspection,

A professional inspector examines the property for:

- Structural issues.

- Plumbing or electrical concerns.

- Roofing or foundation damage.

If significant problems are uncovered, you can renegotiate the price or request the seller to make repairs.

Home Appraisal,

The bank assesses the home's value to confirm it matches the loan amount. If the appraisal comes in lower than expected, you may need to renegotiate or adjust your financing.

Step 3: Finalizing Your Mortgage

Your lender will:

- Verify your financial documentation.

- Approve your loan terms.

- Lock in your mortgage interest rate.

Important: Avoid making large purchases or taking on new debt during this phase, as it could impact your loan approval.

Step 4: Closing the Deal

This is the final stage where everything becomes official. Key steps include:

- ✅ Reviewing and signing the contract: Carefully read all terms and conditions

- ✅ Paying closing costs: Includes taxes, legal fees, lender charges, and insurance

- ✅ Title transfer: Legal ownership of the property is officially transferred to you

Before closing day, conduct a final walkthrough of the home to ensure everything is in the agreed-upon condition.

Step 5: Getting the Keys

Once all documents are signed and payments are completed, you officially own the property. The seller hands over the keys, and you're ready to move in!

Final Thoughts: Your Journey to Homeownership

Buying a home is more than just a transaction; it's a journey. It takes patience, preparation, and the right guidance. With a trusted agent, a clear vision and a step-by-step plan, you can confidently navigate the home-buying process and achieve your dream of homeownership.

Now, it's time to begin the next chapter of your life in a place you can truly call home.

Chapter 5

Avoiding Buyer's Remorse: Common Pitfalls to Watch For

Buyer's remorse is a common experience that can turn an exciting purchase into a regrettable decision. Whether you're buying a car, a house, or even a small gadget, understanding the common pitfalls can help you make confident, informed choices. In this chapter, we will explore key mistakes that lead to regret and provide strategies to avoid them.

1. Rushing the Decision

One of the biggest mistakes buyers make is acting on impulse. Limited-time offers, sales pressure, or excitement can result in a rushed purchase without proper research.

How to Avoid It:

- Take time to compare different options.

- Sleep on major decisions before finalizing them.

- Ensure the purchase aligns with your actual needs and budget.

2. Not Doing Enough Research

Many buyers regret their purchases because they didn't gather enough information, which includes product quality, alternatives, and hidden costs.

How to Avoid It:

- Read product reviews and customer testimonials.

- Compare prices from multiple retailers.

- Research warranties, return policies, and any hidden fees.

3. Falling for Marketing Gimmicks

Companies often use persuasive advertising and psychological tactics to influence buying decisions. Limited-time deals, celebrity endorsements, and "too-good-to-be-true" offers can lead to disappointment.

How to Avoid It:

- Look beyond the marketing and assess the product's actual value.

- Avoid emotional buying, stick to your research and budget.

- Verify if the deal is a genuine discount or just a pricing tactic.

4. Ignoring the Fine Print

Contracts, warranties, and return policies contain important details that can affect your experience. Overlooking these can result in unexpected costs or challenges.

How to Avoid It:

- Read and understand return and exchange policies before buying.

- Be aware of hidden charges, interest rates (for financed items), and warranty exclusions.

- Ask questions if any terms seem unclear or confusing.

5. Letting Emotions Drive the Purchase

Emotional attachment, excitement, or peer pressure can lead to purchasing items that aren't truly necessary, especially with expensive or trendy goods.

How to Avoid It:

- Make a rational decision by listing the pros and cons.

- Set a waiting period before committing to significant purchases.

- Avoid shopping when you're stressed or emotionally vulnerable.

6. Overspending or Ignoring the Budget

Buyers often regret purchases when they later realize it has strained their finances. Overspending can cause anxiety and limit future financial options.

How to Avoid It:

- Set a clear budget before shopping and stick to it.

- Use cash or debit instead of credit to avoid unnecessary debt.

- Consider the long-term financial impact of your purchase.

7. Not Testing the Product or Service First

A common misstep is purchasing something without testing it, leading to dissatisfaction when it doesn't meet expectations.

How to Avoid It:

- Test electronics, appliances, or vehicles before purchase.

- Visit physical stores when possible to inspect quality.

- Check if a free trial or demo is available for digital services.

8. Forgetting About Future Costs

Some items come with ongoing maintenance, subscriptions, or repair expenses that aren't considered initially.

How to Avoid It:

- Account for long-term costs such as upkeep, accessories, and repairs.

- Check whether the product requires costly replacements (e.g., ink cartridges, batteries).

- Be cautious of products tied to expensive ongoing subscriptions.

9. Buying Based on Trends or Peer Pressure

Trends can be enticing, but they often fade quickly, leaving you with items that have little long-term value.

How to Avoid It:

- Make purchases based on personal needs, not popularity.

- Ask yourself whether the item will still be useful in the future.

- Avoid buying just to keep up with others.

10. Neglecting to Ask for Advice

Many buyers make decisions without seeking input from others who have experience with the product or service.

How to Avoid It:

- Ask for recommendations from people who already own the item.

- Consult professionals for major purchases like homes or investments.

- Read independent reviews and product comparison guides.

Final Thoughts

Avoiding buyer's remorse requires thoughtful planning, research, and patience. By being aware of these common pitfalls, you can make informed, confident purchases that lead to long-term satisfaction instead of regret. When in doubt, remember: a well-considered decision is always better than an impulsive one.

Chapter 6

Working with Inspection Companies and Negotiating Repairs

Real estate is one of the largest investments most people will ever make. That's why it's essential to look beyond what's visible at an open house and dig deeper into the true condition of the property. Working with inspection companies plays a critical role in this process. Whether you're buying or selling, understanding the purpose of different inspections and how to act on the findings can help protect your investment and strengthen your negotiating position.

In this chapter, we'll explore the most common types of property inspections, how inspection results affect the deal, and how agents and buyers can work with sellers to request repairs or negotiate credits at closing.

1. Why Inspections Matter

Inspections are more than just a formality; they are a safeguard. A thorough property inspection helps uncover hidden defects, safety hazards, and costly repairs that may not be obvious during a showing. They allow buyers to make informed decisions and provide sellers an opportunity to address issues proactively or adjust the pricing accordingly.

In many cases, the results of a property inspection can directly impact:

- Purchase price

- Repair negotiations

- Closing timeline

- Mortgage approval

- Insurance eligibility

2. Types of Common Real Estate Inspections

1. Home Inspection

This is the most common inspection and is usually conducted shortly after the purchase agreement is signed. A licensed home inspector performs a comprehensive visual assessment of the property's systems and structure.

Typical components reviewed include:

- Foundation and structure.

- Electrical systems.

- HVAC (heating and cooling).

- Plumbing.

- Windows, doors, and insulation.

- Appliances.

- Attic and crawlspace conditions.

- Water heaters and overall safety hazards.

The inspector will produce a detailed report that highlights areas needing attention. This report is the foundation for any repair requests or credits the buyer may seek.

3. Termite or Pest Inspection (Wood-Destroying Organism Report)

This inspection checks for the presence of termites, dry rot, and other wood-destroying pests, which are particularly common in certain climates like California. These pests can cause extensive structural damage, sometimes unnoticed until it's severe.

Many lenders require a termite clearance before funding, especially for government-backed loans like FHA or VA. The report typically shows:

- Active infestations.
- Past damage.
- Areas vulnerable to infestation.

4. Roof Inspection

The roof is one of the most expensive parts of a home to repair or replace. A roof inspection checks the condition of shingles or tiles, flashing, underlayment, and any signs of leaks or poor drainage.

A licensed roofing contractor or specialist can estimate the remaining lifespan of the roof and identify any immediate concerns. Depending on the findings, the buyer may request repairs or negotiate a credit for replacement.

5. Sewer Line or Underground Pipe Inspection

This inspection involves using a camera to check the main sewer line for blockages, cracks, or root intrusion, especially critical in older homes. Sewer line repairs can be costly and are often not covered by homeowners' insurance unless a separate policy is in place.

Underground plumbing issues may not show surface symptoms right away, so this inspection offers valuable peace of mind, particularly in areas with mature landscaping or older infrastructure.

6. Specialized Inspections (As Needed)

Depending on the property's age, location, and condition, additional inspections might be warranted:

- Mold inspection, Chimney inspection.

- Asbestos or lead-based paint (common in pre-1978 homes).

- Pool/spa inspections.

- Geological or soil analysis (for hillside or high-risk zones).

7. Interpreting Reports and Deciding What Matters

Once inspection reports are received, the buyer and agent must determine:

- Which issues are health/safety-related (priority).

- These are minor or cosmetic (low priority).

- Which can be reasonably repaired by the seller.

- Which are better handled after closing with a buyer's credit?

Remember, no home is perfect, even new construction. The goal of inspections is not to nitpick, but to uncover significant issues that affect livability, safety, and long-term costs.

8. Working with Sellers and Listing Agents: Repairs or Credits?

Inspection findings open the door to post-inspection negotiations. Here are the typical paths a buyer can take:

Option 1: Request Repairs Before Closing

The buyer may ask the seller to complete specific repairs. These should be handled by licensed professionals, with receipts provided before the close of escrow.

Option 2: Request a Credit Toward Closing Costs

Instead of making repairs, the seller may agree to offer a credit that helps offset the buyer's closing costs. This option gives the buyer flexibility to manage the repairs on their own timeline and to their own standards.

Option 3: Request a Price Reduction

Some buyers prefer to renegotiate the purchase price instead of asking for repairs or credits, especially if multiple issues were discovered.

Option 4: Walk Away

If the inspection reveals serious problems such as structural damage, unpermitted work, or environmental hazards, the buyer may choose to cancel the contract, assuming they are still within the inspection contingency period.

Pro Tip: Keep negotiations solution-oriented. Instead of simply pointing out problems, propose fair, specific remedies and prioritize health/safety concerns over cosmetic issues.

9. Collaborating with Repair Companies:

In some cases, the buyer's agent may coordinate with licensed contractors to get quotes for necessary repairs. This helps support the buyer's request for credits or price reductions with real, itemized estimates. Collaboration between repair companies, the seller, and the listing agent is essential to:

- Ensure repairs are completed professionally.
- Prevent closing delays.
- Maintain transparency for all parties.

Having reputable contractors in your network as an agent or investor gives you a distinct advantage during these negotiations.

10. Final Thoughts: Inspections Are Your Safety Net:

Working with inspection companies is an essential part of protecting your investment and making an informed purchase decision. Each inspection brings clarity and can reveal deal-breaking red flags or simple fixes that prevent future headaches.

Don't skip inspections to save time or money; doing so can cost you much more in the long run. Instead, embrace this step as your opportunity to:

- Discover the property's true condition.

- Negotiate fair repairs or credits.

- Move forward with peace of mind.

A great real estate agent doesn't just help clients buy property; they guide them through the due diligence that makes it a smart, secure investment.

Part 2

Selling Real Estate

(2/3 Focus)

Chapter 7

Selling with Confidence: Setting the Stage for Success

Selling a home is an important financial decision, and approaching it with confidence can make all the difference. Many sellers feel anxious about the process, but with the right knowledge and preparation, they can position their property for maximum appeal. This chapter explores the key steps to ensuring a successful home sale, from understanding buyer psychology to mastering negotiations and finalizing the deal.

The Seller's Mindset: Overcoming Fear and Uncertainty

The emotional aspects of selling a home can be overwhelming, especially for those who have lived in the property for years. Understanding the market, setting realistic goals, and preparing mentally for negotiations can help sellers overcome uncertainty and approach the sale with confidence. A positive and strategic mindset is essential for making informed decisions and maximizing results.

Preparing the Home for Maximum Appeal

A well-prepared home attracts more buyers and sells faster. Enhancing curb appeal, decluttering interiors, and making minor upgrades can significantly impact a property's desirability. Proper staging techniques create an inviting atmosphere, allowing potential buyers to visualize themselves in the space. A clean, well-maintained home signals value and care, making it more competitive in the market.

The Power of Strategic Marketing

Effective marketing ensures a home reaches the right buyers at the right time. High-quality photography, virtual tours, and compelling listing descriptions help create strong first impressions. Leveraging online platforms, social media, and real estate networks can expand the property's exposure, increasing the chances of attracting serious offers. A targeted marketing approach maximizes visibility and engagement, leading to quicker sales.

Handling Showings and Open Houses with Confidence

Showings and open houses allow buyers to experience the property firsthand. Creating a welcoming and neutral environment helps potential buyers envision themselves living in the home. Sellers should be prepared for last-minute showings, keep the property in top condition, and use feedback from visitors to refine their approach. Properly managed open houses generate interest and increase the likelihood of receiving strong offers.

Navigating Offers, Negotiations, and Closing the Deal

Once offers come in, sellers must assess them carefully and negotiate terms that align with their goals. Evaluating buyer financing, countering strategically, and understanding contingencies play a crucial role in finalizing a successful deal. The closing process involves legal and financial considerations, and being prepared for inspections, appraisals, and paperwork ensures a smooth transaction. Completing the sale with confidence marks the final step in a successful home-selling journey.

Chapter 8

Pricing Strategies That Work: The Art of Valuation

Pricing a home correctly is a delicate balance between market trends, buyer perception, and financial goals. An overpriced home may sit unsold for months, while an underpriced home might result in financial loss. Understanding valuation techniques and strategic pricing methods allows sellers to attract buyers quickly while maximizing their return. This chapter explores the art and science of pricing a home effectively.

Understanding Real Estate Valuation

Determining a home's value requires analyzing various factors, including location, condition, and market trends. Market value, appraised value, and assessed value all play a role in setting a competitive price. Economic conditions, buyer demand, and property features influence how a home is valued in the marketplace. Knowing how to interpret these factors helps sellers price their property accurately.

Conducting a Comparative Market Analysis (CMA)

A comparative market analysis (CMA) helps determine a home's price by evaluating similar properties that have recently sold in the area. Adjustments for square footage, upgrades, and special features refine the pricing strategy. Reviewing current listings and expired properties also provides insights into market trends and competitive pricing. A well-researched CMA ensures a realistic and competitive asking price.

The Psychology of Pricing: How Buyers Perceive Value

Pricing influences buyer perception, and certain psychological tactics can make a home appear more attractive. Numbers ending in "999" or pricing just below major thresholds can encourage more interest. Buyers also respond to price anchoring, where strategic initial pricing leads to stronger negotiations. Creating a sense of urgency and scarcity can drive multiple offers and increase the final sale price.

Pricing Strategies for Different Market Conditions

Real estate markets fluctuate between buyer's markets and seller's markets, and pricing strategies must adapt accordingly. In a seller's market, competitive pricing can lead to bidding wars, while in a buyer's market, pricing aggressively may be necessary to stand out. Seasonal trends also impact pricing, and sellers should time their listings to maximize visibility. Knowing when to adjust pricing based on market feedback is key to maintaining buyer interest.

Adjusting Price Based on Market Feedback and Performance

If a home remains unsold for an extended period, price adjustments may be necessary. Tracking buyer interest, reviewing showing feedback, and analyzing comparable sales help determine whether a price reduction is needed. Gradual adjustments can prevent a home from appearing stale on the market. Re-marketing the property with a fresh strategy can help reinvigorate interest and lead to a successful sale.

Special Pricing Strategies for Unique Situations

Certain properties, such as luxury homes, fixer-uppers, and distressed sales, require specialized pricing strategies. Luxury homes benefit from prestige pricing and targeted marketing, while fixer-uppers must be priced to attract investors and renovation buyers. Urgent sales, such as relocations or estate settlements, often require a balance between speed and value. Understanding the nuances of different property types ensures sellers achieve the best possible outcome.

Chapter 9

Marketing Magic: How to Make Your Home Stand Out

Selling a home is not just about listing it; it's about making it irresistible to buyers. In a competitive market, standing out is crucial, and that requires a strategic marketing approach. This chapter delves into the essential elements of marketing a home from visual presentation to pricing, online exposure, and traditional advertising. By mastering these techniques, you can attract the right buyers and maximize the value of your property.

Creating a Strong First Impression

First impressions last. A home that looks attractive from the outset has a better chance of capturing buyer interest and commanding a higher price.

Curb Appeal: The Exterior Matters

The exterior of a home sets the tone for what's inside. A well-manicured lawn, trimmed hedges, and colorful flowers create an inviting look. Freshly painted doors, updated house numbers, and polished fixtures signal that the home is well-maintained. The driveway and walkway should be clean and free of cracks, and outdoor lighting can add charm, especially for evening viewings.

Interior Presentation: Staging for Success

Staging transforms a home into a welcoming space that buyers can envision themselves living in. Decluttering and deep cleaning make rooms feel spacious and bright. Neutral color palettes appeal to a broader audience, while strategic furniture placement enhances flow and functionality. Thoughtful touches like fresh flowers, soft music, and subtle scents can evoke a sense of comfort and luxury.

Photography and Virtual Tours: The Key to Online Attraction

The vast majority of homebuyers start their search online, making visual representation one of the most critical aspects of marketing.

Why Professional Photography Matters

High-resolution images with proper lighting make a listing stand out. Professional photographers know how to highlight a home's best features, from expansive windows to intricate architectural details. Well-composed photos create an emotional connection, prompting buyers to schedule a viewing.

The Impact of Virtual Tours

Virtual tours offer an immersive experience that allows buyers to explore a home remotely. 3D tours provide a realistic walkthrough, while drone footage showcases expansive properties and desirable neighborhoods. Video tours add a dynamic element, giving buyers a guided experience of the home's layout and special features.

Crafting the Perfect Listing Description

A well-written listing description can turn an ordinary property into a dream home.

Writing with Emotion and Clarity

Descriptions should go beyond listing features; they should tell a story. Instead of stating, "Three-bedroom home with a large backyard," describe how "this charming three-bedroom home offers a spacious backyard perfect for summer barbecues and relaxing evenings under the stars."

Avoiding Common Listing Mistakes

Exaggerated claims or generic language can deter buyers. Overuse of phrases like "must-see" or "great location" without specifics can make a listing feel unoriginal. Instead, highlight unique elements, such as "a sun-drenched breakfast nook with garden views" or "a spa-inspired master bathroom with a deep soaking tub."

Setting the Right Price to Attract Buyers

Pricing is a balancing act. A well-priced home attracts multiple offers, while an overpriced home may sit on the market for months.

Understanding Market Comparisons

A comparative market analysis (CMA) compares recent sales of similar homes in the area. This analysis helps determine a competitive price that aligns with current market trends.

The Risks of Overpricing

Homes priced too high discourage buyers and may require price reductions, which can make a property seem undesirable. A slightly lower, competitive price can create urgency and lead to bidding wars, ultimately increasing the final sale price.

Using Digital Marketing to Maximize Exposure

Modern home sales rely heavily on digital marketing. Reaching buyers where they spend most of their time on social media and real estate websites can significantly impact sales.

Social Media Strategies

Platforms like Facebook, Instagram, and TikTok offer a direct way to showcase listings. Engaging content, including behind-the-scenes home tours and interactive Q&A sessions, can attract potential buyers.

Listing on Multiple Platforms

Using major listing sites such as Zillow, Redfin, and Realtor.com ensures a wider reach. Optimizing listings with relevant keywords improves search visibility, increasing the chances of attracting serious buyers.

Traditional Marketing Strategies That Still Work

While digital marketing is essential, traditional methods still play a vital role in selling a home.

The Power of Open Houses

An open house allows multiple buyers to view a home in a relaxed setting. A well-organized open house with refreshments, informative brochures, and guided tours can generate serious interest.

Print Advertising and Local Networking

Printed flyers, brochures, and direct mail campaigns can reach buyers who may not be actively searching online. Local networking, including real estate agent collaborations and community events can also attract the right audience.

Tracking Your Marketing Success

Evaluating marketing performance helps identify what's working and where adjustments are needed.

Analyzing Buyer Engagement

Monitoring online listing views, social media interactions, and open house attendance provides insights into buyer interest. Low engagement may indicate the need for refreshed photos, revised descriptions, or pricing adjustments.

When to Make Adjustments

If a home isn't receiving offers, tweaking the marketing approach can reignite interest. Updating the listing, enhancing staging, or re-evaluating the price can lead to a faster sale.

By implementing these marketing strategies, sellers can ensure their home stands out and attracts the right buyers.

Chapter 10

Partnering for Profit: Choosing the Right Agent to List Your Home

A knowledgeable real estate agent can make the difference between a smooth, profitable home sale and a stressful, prolonged process. This chapter covers how to find, evaluate, and work with the right agent to achieve the best results.

Why a Good Agent Matters?

The right agent brings expertise, negotiation skills, and a network of buyers and professionals.

The Role of a Listing Agent

A listing agent provides market analysis, marketing strategies, and pricing advice. They coordinate showings, negotiate offers, and guide sellers through the closing process.

How an Agent Affects Your Bottom Line

A skilled agent knows how to price a home to maximize value while ensuring a quick sale. Poor pricing or weak negotiation skills can result in lost profits.

How to Find a Top-Performing Agent

Choosing an agent requires research, referrals, and direct evaluation.

Where to Look for the Best Agents

Online reviews, personal recommendations, and attending open houses provide insight into an agent's reputation and performance.

Checking an Agent's Track Record

A strong sales history, short listing-to-sale timeframes, and positive client testimonials indicate a reliable agent.

Interviewing Potential Agents

Meeting multiple agents before choosing one allows for comparison.

Important Questions to Ask

Questions about pricing strategy, marketing plans, and experience in the local market reveal the agent's approach.

Assessing Communication Style

Clear and frequent communication is essential. Agents should provide updates, answer questions, and address concerns promptly.

Understanding Real Estate Agent Fees and Contracts

Knowing how commissions work and what services are included prevents misunderstandings.

How the Commission Works

Most agents earn a percentage of the sale price, typically 5–6%. Some offer flexible or reduced rates.

What's Included in the Fee?

Photography, marketing, negotiation, and paperwork handling are often part of an agent's services.

Red Flags to Watch for When Choosing an Agent:

Certain warning signs indicate that an agent may not be a good fit.

Overpromising and Underperforming:

An agent who guarantees an unrealistically high sale price may be setting false expectations.

Lack of Experience in Your Market

Agents unfamiliar with local trends may struggle to price and market a home effectively.

Working Effectively with Your Agent:

A successful partnership with an agent leads to a smoother sale.

Establishing Clear Expectations:

Setting communication guidelines and marketing strategies upfront ensures alignment.

Trusting Their Expertise

Relying on the agent's knowledge while staying informed helps facilitate a successful transaction.

Choosing the right agent is a key factor in selling a home quickly and at the best price. With the right partnership, the selling process becomes more efficient and rewarding.

Chapter 11

Sealing the Deal: Negotiating and Closing with Ease

The final stages of a real estate transaction are often the most crucial. Negotiating the right deal and successfully closing it can determine whether you walk away with a profitable outcome or a deal fraught with unexpected costs and complications. Mastering this phase requires a combination of skill, market awareness, and strategic planning. This chapter explores the nuances of negotiation, the key steps involved in closing a deal, and how to navigate common challenges that arise along the way.

The Art of Negotiation in Real Estate

Negotiation is at the heart of every real estate transaction. Whether you are buying or selling a property, understanding how to engage in effective discussions can make a significant difference in the final terms. Successful negotiation is not about winning or losing, but about creating a deal that satisfies both parties while securing the most favorable terms for yourself. Emotional intelligence, preparation, and a thorough knowledge of market conditions play a critical role in shaping the negotiation process.

Buyers often aim to negotiate a lower price, request repairs, or obtain favorable closing terms, while sellers strive to maximize their return and minimize concessions. Knowing how to counter an offer without driving the other party away is essential. Factors such as timing, leverage, and competition all influence the success of negotiations. This section will delve into proven strategies to create win-win situations and ensure a smooth transition toward closing.

Crafting the Perfect Offer and Counteroffer Strategy

Making a compelling offer is one of the most strategic moves in a real estate deal. For buyers, a strong offer not only includes a competitive price but also considers contingencies, deposit amounts, and closing timelines. For sellers, reviewing and countering offers requires careful analysis to ensure they get the best possible deal without losing a potential buyer.

Understanding the elements that make an offer attractive can give you a competitive edge. A well-prepared buyer will have financing in place, understand the property's true value, and be ready to make adjustments to meet the seller's expectations. Similarly, a seller should anticipate potential counteroffers and be prepared to negotiate terms such as price adjustments, closing costs, or repair credits.

Overcoming Common Negotiation Hurdles

Every real estate deal comes with its own set of challenges. A buyer might feel uncertain after an inspection reveals unexpected issues, or a seller might hesitate to lower the price despite market conditions suggesting otherwise. Appraisal gaps, financing contingencies, and last-minute changes from either party can delay or even derail a deal.

Navigating these challenges requires flexibility and problem-solving skills. If an appraisal comes in lower than expected, both parties must decide whether to renegotiate the price, make up the difference, or walk away from the deal. If financing falls through, alternative arrangements must be made quickly. Effective communication and a willingness to compromise often make the difference between a successful closing and a lost opportunity.

The Closing Process: What to Expect

Closing a real estate deal involves multiple steps, each requiring attention to detail. Buyers and sellers must work with agents, attorneys, lenders, and title companies to finalize the transaction. During this phase, all legal and financial documents are reviewed, and any remaining conditions must be met.

A closing disclosure is provided to the buyer, outlining all costs and financial details. Both parties will need to complete necessary paperwork, transfer ownership, and ensure all agreed-upon conditions have been satisfied. Unexpected delays can arise from title issues, loan approval holdups, or errors in the documentation, making it crucial to stay informed and proactive. Once all requirements are met, the property officially changes hands, and the deal is sealed.

Conclusion

Negotiating and closing a real estate deal requires careful planning, patience, and the ability to navigate unexpected obstacles. Whether you are buying or selling, understanding the dynamics of negotiation and the intricacies of the closing process can help you secure a smooth and profitable transaction. By mastering these skills, you can confidently move through the final stages of a deal with ease and efficiency.

Chapter 12

Turning Sales into Success: Maximizing Profits from Your Property

Selling a property is not just about finding a buyer; it's about securing the highest possible return on your investment. Many factors influence the final sale price, from the way a property is presented to the prevailing market conditions at the time of sale. Success in real estate sales comes from a well-planned strategy that includes accurate pricing, effective marketing, and skillful negotiation. This chapter explores how to optimize every aspect of the sales process to maximize profits while ensuring a smooth transaction.

Pricing Your Property for Maximum Profit

One of the most critical decisions when selling a property is setting the right price. Overpricing can drive potential buyers away, while underpricing can leave money on the table. The key is to analyze current market trends, compare similar properties, and establish a competitive yet profitable price point.

Market conditions play a significant role in pricing strategy. In a seller's market, where demand exceeds supply, properties can often sell above the asking price. In contrast, in a buyer's market, sellers may need to be more flexible with pricing to attract interest.

Understanding the psychology behind pricing, such as the impact of round numbers and psychological pricing tactics, can also give sellers an advantage in attracting the right buyers.

Preparing Your Property for a High-Value Sale

The presentation of a property can significantly affect its perceived value. Buyers are more likely to pay a premium for a well-maintained, aesthetically pleasing home. Staging, decluttering, and minor renovations can enhance a property's appeal and help justify a higher asking price.

Simple upgrades such as fresh paint, modern lighting, and updated fixtures can make a noticeable difference. More substantial renovations, like kitchen and bathroom improvements, often yield greater returns. The goal is to create an inviting atmosphere where buyers can envision themselves living, ultimately increasing their willingness to meet or exceed the asking price.

Strategic Marketing to Attract High-Value Buyers

A strong marketing strategy ensures maximum exposure and attracts serious buyers. Traditional methods, such as open houses and print advertising, have evolved to include digital tools that expand reach and engagement. High-quality photography, virtual tours, and targeted online advertising can dramatically increase interest in a property.

The listing description should emphasize the property's strongest features while being clear and accurate about its specifications. Leveraging social media, real estate platforms, and email marketing also helps reach the ideal audience. A well-crafted marketing plan positions the property as a valuable asset, leading to quicker sales and higher offers.

Negotiating Offers to Maximize Profitability

Receiving multiple offers can be advantageous, but selecting the right one requires careful evaluation. A higher offer isn't always the best if it comes with excessive contingencies or financing risks. Sellers must assess the strength of each offer based on factors such as buyer pre-approval, cash versus financed deals, and proposed closing timelines.

Effective negotiation helps ensure that the seller secures the most favorable terms. Counteroffers, seller concessions, and the removal of contingencies can all be used to improve the final deal. Knowing when to push for better terms and when to accept a strong offer is a vital skill that contributes to maximum profitability.

Investing the Profits for Long-Term Wealth

Once a property is sold, the next step is determining how to reinvest the profits. Some sellers choose to remain in real estate by purchasing rental properties, flipping homes, or investing in real estate investment trusts (REITs). Others may diversify into stocks, bonds, or alternative assets. Thoughtful financial planning ensures that profits from real estate contribute to long-term wealth rather than being spent impulsively.

Conclusion

Selling a property for maximum profit requires thoughtful planning, market knowledge, and strategic execution. By setting the right price, enhancing the property's presentation, leveraging strong marketing tactics, and negotiating skillfully, sellers can turn a standard transaction into a significant financial success. Mastering these principles empowers real estate sellers to build lasting wealth and open doors to future investment opportunities.

Chapter 13

Working with Escrow, Title Companies and Understanding Property Vesting

In any real estate transaction, whether residential, commercial, or investment, the processes that take place behind the scenes are just as important as the ones in front. Understanding how escrow and title companies operate, how to properly choose one, and how property ownership (vesting) is structured can help avoid costly mistakes, reduce stress, and ensure a smooth closing experience.

This chapter breaks down the critical roles played by escrow and title companies, how to properly select one for your transaction, and why understanding title vesting and property liens is essential for long-term ownership success.

1. The Role of Escrow and Title Companies

What Is Escrow?

Escrow is a neutral third party that holds funds and documents during a real estate transaction until all terms of the purchase agreement are fulfilled. Think of escrow as the secure "middle ground" where both buyer and seller can safely exchange what's required to close the deal, free of bias and protected by regulation.

The escrow officer's responsibilities include:

- Holding the buyer's earnest money deposit.

- Ensuring all paperwork is signed and in order.

- Confirming loan funding and payoff amounts.

- Managing the disbursement of funds.

- Recording the deed after closing.

What Is a Title Company?

The title company is responsible for researching the property's ownership history and confirming that the seller has the legal right to transfer ownership. It also issues title insurance, which protects the buyer and lender from future claims or legal issues related to ownership, liens, or undiscovered heirs.

Services provided by the title company include:

- Performing a title search to verify the property is free of encumbrances.

- Issuing a title report (also known as a preliminary title report).

- Offering title insurance policies to both buyers and lenders.

- Recording the deed and mortgage at the local county recorder's office.

2. Choosing the Right Escrow or Title Company

Local, Regional, or National: Which One Is Best?

There's no one-size-fits-all answer. Depending on your needs, you might choose:

Local title/escrow firms: These often provide a more personalized experience and maintain strong relationships with nearby lenders, agents, and municipalities.

Regional companies: Offer a balance of local expertise and broader service coverage.

National title companies: Provide consistency and standardization, especially helpful in multi-state transactions.

Key Criteria to Consider

When selecting a company, look for the following:

Cost

Fees for escrow and title services can vary significantly based on location and transaction size. Always request a breakdown of costs in advance. Some states have standardized rates, while others allow for negotiation.

Customer Service

Choose a company known for responsiveness and dependability. A good title or escrow officer is proactive, organized, and communicates clearly, especially during time-sensitive stages like closing.

Industry Expertise

If your transaction involves special circumstances (e.g., foreclosures, investment properties, or commercial real estate), select a firm experienced in those areas. Specialized knowledge can prevent delays and costly errors.

3. Understanding Title Vesting: How You Own the Property Matters

What Is Vesting?

Vesting refers to how property ownership is legally held. This has major implications for estate planning, taxes, legal liability, and future sales or transfers of the property. Many buyers overlook this, but it's one of the most important decisions you'll make during escrow.

Common Forms of Vesting:

Individual Ownership

Property is owned solely by one person. This is straightforward but may require probate if the owner passes away without a will or trust.

Joint Tenancy with Right of Survivorship

Two or more people own the property equally. If one owner passes away, the property automatically transfers to the surviving owner(s), regardless of the deceased's will.

Tenancy in Common

Two or more owners can hold unequal interests. Upon death, ownership passes according to the individual's will or estate, not automatically to the other owner(s).

Community Property

In states like California, this is available to married couples. Each spouse owns an equal share, and the property can be passed on through a will or trust.

Living Trust

The property is owned by a trust, with instructions for management and distribution upon the owner's death. This helps avoid probate and offers greater privacy.

LLC or Corporation

Often used by real estate investors or developers, ownership under an LLC offers asset protection and potential tax advantages. However, it requires ongoing maintenance and may complicate financing.

Pro Tip: Always consult a legal or tax advisor to determine the vesting option that best suits your goals, especially if you have a complex estate, business interests, or plan to pass property to heirs.

4. Title Searches, Liens, and Due Diligence

Before closing on any property, it's essential to confirm there are no hidden legal or financial issues that could arise after the transaction.

What a Title Search Reveals:

- Current and previous owners (chain of title).

- Existing mortgages or liens.

- Property tax delinquencies.

- Easements or restrictions (e.g., shared driveways or utility access).

- Legal judgments or bankruptcy claims against prior owners.

A clean title ensures you're buying a property free from legal entanglements. If issues are discovered, the title company will attempt to resolve them before closing. If they cannot be resolved, you may choose to walk away or renegotiate the terms.

Title Insurance: A Critical Safety Net

There are two main types of title insurance:

Owner's Policy: Protects you, the buyer, from future claims.

Lender's Policy: Required by most lenders to safeguard their financial interest.

This one-time premium offers peace of mind and long-term financial protection after the sale closes.

5. Final Thoughts: Protecting Your Investment

Working with the right escrow and title company, choosing the appropriate form of vesting, and conducting proper due diligence are essential to a successful real estate transaction. These "invisible" steps often determine whether a deal is smooth or problematic and how protected you'll be long after closing.

By taking the time to understand these processes and make informed decisions, you position yourself and your clients for long-term success and peace of mind in any real estate venture.

Chapter 14

1031 Exchange

"The Secret Weapon of Real Estate Investors"

A Smarter Way to Grow Wealth

If you've been in real estate for any amount of time, you've probably heard this golden rule: It's not just about what you make, it's about what you keep. The 1031 Exchange is a perfect example of that principle in action.

Picture this: you sell an investment property for a nice profit. Now, imagine being able to take every dollar of that profit and reinvest it directly into your next deal without handing a chunk of it over to the IRS. That's the power of a 1031 Exchange. It's a tax strategy that's been quietly helping investors grow faster, smarter, and more efficiently for decades.

In this chapter, we'll break down the 1031 Exchange so it actually makes sense, no legal jargon, no confusing tax talk. Just real-world knowledge you can use to make better decisions and build more wealth through real estate.

What Exactly Is a 1031 Exchange?

At its core, a 1031 Exchange is like a legal "swap" where you're exchanging one investment property for another without cashing out and triggering capital gains tax. It's not about avoiding taxes; it's about deferring them. You'll pay them eventually, but not today. And that means you get to reinvest your full gains into something bigger or better right now.

Let's say you bought a rental home years ago for $300,000, and today it's worth $600,000. If you sell, you'd normally owe taxes on that $300,000 in profit. But if you do a 1031 Exchange, you can roll that entire $600,000 into another property and pay no taxes at the time of sale. That's a massive win.

Why Investors Love the 1031 Exchange

The 1031 Exchange isn't just some technical tax rule; it's a powerful growth tool. Investors use it to:

- Keep more of their profit working for them.
- Buy bigger, better, or more profitable properties.
- Move their investments to better markets or asset classes.
- Combine or divide properties to meet their goals.

It's all about building momentum. The more capital you reinvest, the faster you can scale your portfolio. Over time, this kind of leverage can completely transform your financial trajectory.

What Does "Like-Kind" Really Mean?

One of the most confusing parts of the 1031 Exchange is the term "like-kind." But here's the truth: it's more flexible than it sounds.

You don't have to swap an apartment building for another apartment building. As long as both properties are used for investment or business purposes, they're generally considered like-kind. For example:

- A rental house for a strip mall.

- A piece of raw land for a warehouse.

- An Airbnb unit for a commercial office building.

What you can't do is exchange a personal-use property like your primary residence or a vacation home you don't rent out. But if the property produces income and is held for investment, chances are it qualifies.

The Clock Starts Ticking: Know the Deadlines

A 1031 Exchange isn't something you can procrastinate on. The IRS has strict deadlines, and missing them means you lose the tax benefits.

First, you have 45 days after selling your property to identify potential replacements. That means putting them in writing, no "I'll figure it out later" allowed.

Most people follow the Three-Property Rule (name up to three options). There's also the 200% Rule and 95% Rule, which are more advanced and used in specific scenarios.

Second, you have 180 days from the date of sale to close on the new property. And no, the 45 days aren't in addition to the 180, they're included. You've got six months total.

Why You Need a Qualified Intermediary (QI)

Here's a deal-breaker: you can't touch the sale money. Not even for a second. If the funds land in your hands even by accident, your exchange is disqualified, and you'll owe taxes immediately.

That's why you need a Qualified Intermediary (QI). They're the third-party professional who holds the money, prepares the paperwork, and ensures everything remains compliant.

A reputable QI will:

- Safely hold your funds in escrow.

- Prepare the legal exchange documents.

- Coordinate with your title and escrow teams.

- Help you meet the IRS's rules and deadlines.

Just make sure you choose an experienced and trustworthy QI; not all of them are created equal.

Here's How a 1031 Exchange Actually Works:

- You sell your investment property, and the sale proceeds go directly to your QI.

- Within 45 days, you identify new properties you're considering

- You sign a purchase agreement for one of those properties.

- You close the deal within 180 days of your original sale.

- You report everything on IRS Form 8824 when you file your taxes.

That's it in theory. In practice, it takes planning, coordination, and a reliable team.

Advanced Moves: Reverse and Improvement Exchanges

Sometimes the timing doesn't line up; maybe you find your dream property before you sell your current one. That's where a Reverse Exchange comes in. It lets you buy first and sell later. It's more complex and requires expert handling.

There's also the Improvement Exchange, where you use your exchange funds to fix up or build out the replacement property during the exchange period. Again, this is totally doable, but you need a professional to structure it correctly.

Mistakes That Can Cost You

The 1031 Exchange is a powerful tool, but it's not forgiving. Here are a few of the most costly missteps:

- Missing the 45- or 180-day deadlines.

- Listing the wrong property on your identification form.

- Trying to exchange a personal-use property.

- Receiving the funds yourself instead of using a QI.

- Reinvesting only part of the proceeds creates a taxable portion known as "boot".

These are easy mistakes to make and expensive ones. Always plan and work with a qualified professional.

Real-Life Success: Mark's $5M Journey

Mark started small, just a $200,000 rental home in a quiet neighborhood. Over the years, he used 1031 Exchanges to keep trading up. Each time, he avoided taxes and reinvested everything. Twenty years later, he owns a real estate portfolio worth over $5 million and hasn't paid a dime in capital gains tax yet. That's the magic of deferred growth.

When a 1031 Exchange Doesn't Make Sense

Sometimes, it's better to skip the 1031 Exchange. Maybe you want to cash out, or maybe you've got losses to offset gains this year. In those situations, paying the tax now might actually be smarter.

It's not always black and white; this is where a good CPA or tax advisor is essential.

Final Thoughts: Know the Rules, Use the Tool

The 1031 Exchange isn't a loophole; it's a smart, legal tool, but only if you use it correctly. When executed properly, it can supercharge your investment strategy and help you build real wealth over time.

But don't try to wing it. Surround yourself with the right people: a great agent, a savvy CPA, and a trusted QI. When the pieces are in place, the 1031 Exchange becomes one of the most powerful tools in your real estate toolkit.

****

Real Estate Resources

A curated list of trusted resources to support buyers, sellers, and investors throughout their real estate journey:

Home Buying Guides

- Buyer's Guide – California Association of Realtors

- Home Buyer's Guide – Realtor.com

- Consumer Guide: Buying Your First Home – NAR

- Buying a Home – U.S. Department of Housing and Urban Development

- Step-by-Step Home Buying Process – Credit.org

- Buying a House: Tools and Resources – Consumer Finance

Specialty Buyer Resources

- VA Home Loan Guaranty Buyer's Guide

- Single Family Housing Guaranteed Loan Program – USDA

- Affordable Mortgage Lending Center Guide – FDIC

- Step-by-Step Mortgage Guide – FHFA

Educational Tools

- Home View Homebuyer Education – Fannie Mae

- Handouts for Buyers – National Association of Realtors

- Home Buyer's and Seller's Guide to Radon – EPA

Financial Tools

- Mortgage Calculator

- Bankrate – Mortgage & Financial Tools

- Home Mortgage Disclosure Act (HMDA) – FFIEC

Investing Resources

- Real Estate Investment Trusts (REITs) – Investor.gov